discovermore

Economics in Your Community

Saving and Spending

Sloane Wilden

Britannica Educational Publishing

IN ASSOCIATION WITH

THE ROSEN PUBLISHING GROUP

Published in 2024 by The Rosen Publishing Group, Inc.
2544 Clinton Street, Buffalo, NY 14224

Editor: Brianna Propis
Book Design: Michael Flynn

Photo Credits: Cover file404/Shutterstock.com; (series background) Dai Yim/Shutterstock.com; p. 4 sblaster/Shutterstock.com; p. 5 ChristianChan/Shutterstock.com; p. 7 (top) Kdonmuang/Shutterstock.com; p. 7 (bottom) Viktoriia Hnatiuk/Shutterstock.com; p. 8 Andrey Arkusha/Shutterstock.com; p. 9 TORWAISTUDIO/Shutterstock.com; p. 10 Prostock-studio/Shutterstock.com; p. 11 Alrandir/Shutterstock.com; p. 12 Stanislaw Mikulski/Shutterstock.com; p. 13 Evgeny Karandaev/Shutterstock.com; p. 14 Serhii Bobyk/Shutterstock.com; p. 15 fizkes/Shutterstock.com; p. 16 Ruth Black/Shutterstock.com; p. 17 Ultraskrip/Shutterstock.com; p. 18 Lutsenko_Oleksandr/Shutterstock.com; p. 19 Alliance Images/Shutterstock.com; p. 20 Hi my name is Jacco/Shutterstock.com; p. 21 Billion Photos/Shutterstock.com; p. 22 Vitalii Vodolazskyi/Shutterstock.com; pp. 23, 29(bottom) Monkey Business Images/Shutterstock.com; p. 24 Prostock-studio/Shutterstock.com; p. 25 Elle Aon/Shutterstock.com; p. 26 GG Photos/Shutterstock.com; p. 27 addkm/Shutterstock.com; p. 29 (top) Andrey_Popov/Shutterstock.com.

Library of Congress Cataloging-in-Publication Data

Names: Wilden, Sloane, author.
Title: Saving and spending / Sloane Wilden.
Description: Buffalo : Britannica Educational Publishing, [2024] | Series: Discover more: Economics in your community | Includes bibliographical references and index.
Identifiers: LCCN 2023030638 | ISBN 9781641900393 (library binding) | ISBN 9781641900386 (paperback) | ISBN 9781641900409 (ebook)
Subjects: LCSH: Finance, Personal--Juvenile literature. | Money--Juvenile literature. | Saving and investment--Juvenile literature.
Classification: LCC HG173.8 .W55 2024 | DDC 332.024--dc23/eng/20230706
LC record available at https://lccn.loc.gov/2023030638

Manufactured in the United States of America

CPSIA Compliance Information: Batch #CWBRIT24. For further information contact Rosen Publishing at 1-800-237-9932.

Contents

To Spend or Not To Spend

Your parents just gave you $10 for your weekly allowance. They instruct you to save some, spend some, and donate some.

When you save money, you put your money away for future use. People put their saved money into different places, like a jar or a bank account.

Regularly saving small amounts of money can add up to a substantial amount.

Giving to charity helps others meet their needs. Some of the largest charities in America are Feeding America, which provides food to those who cannot afford it, and St. Jude Children's Research Hospital, dedicated to helping children with cancer or other diseases.

You spend money when you buy goods and services. Goods are things you can touch, like clothing, jewelry, or food. Services are things that people do for you, like cutting your hair, serving you at a restaurant, or fixing your car.

Donating your money is using your money to help others. Some people don't have enough money to pay for food, clothes, or housing. Donations can be in the form of money that enables people to afford these things, the goods themselves, or they can be volunteered services.

Consider This

When people have an allowance or a job, they earn a certain amount of money that helps them pay for things. How does the amount a person earns affect what they can spend their money on?

Money Origins

A source of income, such as an allowance, helps people pay for things they need or want. Income is money that you receive. You can get income as gifts, like birthday and holiday gifts. You can also earn income by working.

Suppose you have a job as a babysitter and you're paid $12.00 for each hour you work. After working four hours, your income is $48.00.

A wage or salary is money paid for doing a job. Wages are fixed amounts you earn each hour. You receive a wage for babysitting. A salary is the amount a person earns every year.

compare and contrast

Being paid "minimum wage" is the least amount of money that a business or company can legally pay someone to work per hour. Some states in America, such as California, pay $15.50 for minimum wage. Others, like Georgia, pay $7.25. Compare and contrast how a higher and lower wage could affect the workers and their companies.

A child might earn an allowance for helping with household chores, such as cleaning rooms in the house, walking their family pet, or washing the dishes.

Teenagers can earn money in many ways, such as by babysitting, delivering pizza, raking and mowing lawns, or working as a cashier in a grocery store.

Decisions, Decisions

Income is used to pay for expenses, which are goods and services that cost money. You choose your expenses based on your needs and wants. Needs are things you must have to live, such as food and clothes. Wants are things you would like to have but don't need.

Some expenses are fixed, which means they don't change. A person who rents or owns a home agrees to pay the same amount to live there each month. A person with a car payment pays a fixed amount each month for the car.

Spending money means a person has to make decisions. They might decide to walk somewhere instead of driving to save money on gas, or to cook dinner at home instead of eating at a restaurant to save money on food.

The price of food may vary depending on where you buy it from. Buying fruit at a farmer's market may be more expensive, but fresher. A grocery store's fruit may be cheaper, but not as fresh.

Some expenses are variable, which means they can change. Food, clothes, and gas are variable expenses. Each month, these amounts can be different. Say a person chooses to walk or ride their bicycle more and drive less in the summer. They will spend less on gas during these months and save money.

Consider This

A receipt is a physical or digital record of how much you paid for something. How might saving receipts help a person track their spending?

Maybe Another Time

You want to buy a new video game console that was just released. But what if it costs more money than you have? How can you buy the game?

Many people choose to save a fixed amount each month in order to reach their **financial goals**. If you know how much the console costs, you can save a little bit each month until you have that amount.

Your needs and wants help determine your financial goals. If your family likes travelling, being able to visit new places around the country or world may be a financial goal.

During a winter storm, a branch might unexpectedly fall on top of your parents' car and damage the windshield. They may need to use money set aside to fix the surprise incident.

Your savings plan may change if your goals change. You may choose to save more of your allowance each month to buy the game console sooner. You may also decide you want to buy another game as well so you need to save even more.

Savings also come in handy for unexpected emergencies. A person may need to pay to fix a broken windshield or other unexpected expenses.

WORD WISE

FINANCIAL GOALS ARE THINGS YOU WANT TO BUY IN THE FUTURE, OR A CERTAIN AMOUNT OF MONEY YOU WANT TO SAVE BY A CERTAIN DATE.

Financial Goals

The amount of money you have, or your totals savings, grows when you consistently set money aside. If you save $3.00 each month, you will have $36.00 in savings after one year. If you save $4.00 each month instead, you will have $48.00 after one year. When you save more money each month, your total savings grow even faster.

Saving more money per month, or saving $2.00 every two weeks instead of every four, can help you to reach your financial goals faster.

Reaching a goal means working toward something within a set amount of time and accomplishing it. Some goals take longer to achieve than others, depending on what you need to do to reach them.

Certain financial goals require longer plans than others. Short-term goals, like buying a new video game, take less than six months to reach. Long-term goals can take years. Paying for college, a home, or a car are long-term goals.

When you reach a goal, you feel good inside because it's an accomplishment. You can buy something you've been saving your money for.

Consider This

"Pay yourself first" is a strategy used by people to remind themselves to set money aside before spending any. Why might this be a useful strategy?

Planning Purchases

To help keep track of income and expenses many people make a budget, or financial plan. If income equals expenses, then the budget is balanced. A teenager's monthly budget is balanced when she spends and earns the same amount. Her fixed expenses include a set amount for savings.

Not all budgets are balanced. If income is greater than expenses, there is extra money for savings and financial goals. If expenses are greater than income, people are in debt, or owe money.

Some expenses—like entertainment—are a want, not a need. We spend money on them because they make us feel happy.

Being financially responsible means you are aware of the expenses you need to pay, and that you are earning enough income to pay them with.

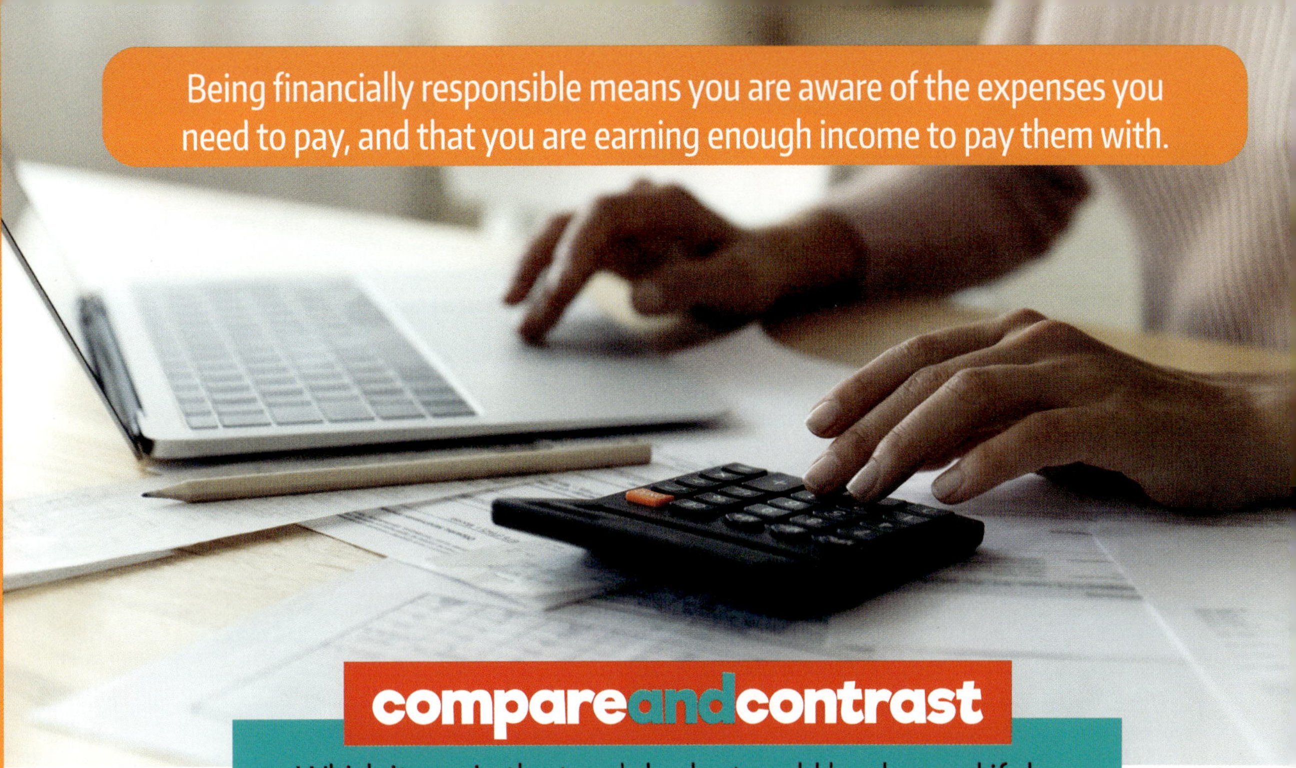

compare and contrast

Which items in the teen's budget could be changed if she wanted to save more money? Which ones stay the same?

Income		Fixed Expenses		Variable Expenses	
Allowance	$15.00	Cell Phone Bill	$20.00	Eating Out	$10.00
Walking Dogs	$25.00	Subway Ticket	$30.00	Entertainment (concerts, movies, games)	$15.00
Babysitting	$60.00	Savings	$20.00	Clothes	$20.00
Gifts	$20.00				
Total	**$120.00**	**Total**	**$70.00**	**Total**	**$45.00**

Total Income: $120.00
Total Expenses: $115.00

I'm Busy Budgeting!

Budgeting can help a person navigate their short-term and long-term financial goals. Suppose a high-school girl wants to buy a ticket to a concert, but the ticket costs more than her total savings. How can she use her budget to reach her goal?

She has a few choices. The teen can earn more income, have fewer expenses, or do both to save extra money. She can walk dogs or babysit more often. She can also spend less money on variable expenses, such as eating out and buying clothes.

You can earn more income by selling old clothes, hosting a bake sale, or walking dogs in your neighborhood—but make sure to advertise so customers can find you!

Keeping your receipts is a useful tool when tracking your expenses. They'll also come in handy if you want to return or exchange an item you bought!

Paying your bills and saving money means making choices. You must record the right amounts for income and expenses to understand your choices. A budget is then used to help you calculate and navigate your financial goals.

Consider This

Some income and expenses change every month. You may spend more money on food or clothing than you usually do, or an unexpected expense might pop up. How can tracking income and expenses for several months help you to predict your future income and expenses?

Clever Cash

If you're looking for a new pair of jeans, you may notice the same pair can be found online and in a store at the mall for different prices. Comparing prices helps you make the best purchase. Total prices of online orders often include shipping costs. You may also find similar goods and services that cost less. For example, many grocery stores have their own brand of packaged foods that cost less than the more popular national brands.

Although it may take time, comparing prices and searching for sales will save you money in the long run.

Online coupons can be found on the internet, such as on the website you're planning to make a purchase from—just be sure to keep an eye out for scams. Someone could charge you money or steal your information for a coupon that doesn't work.

Coupons and rebates help you to pay less than the full price. A coupon gives you a certain amount off the price. You can find coupons online, in the mail, and in stores. A rebate gives you money back for something you already bought.

Smart spending includes having a plan when buying something. A person might spend over their budget if they buy too many things without planning ahead.

Consider This

Peer pressure is when friends try to influence you, such as convincing you to buy something. How could you protect yourself from being peer pressured into buying something you don't need?

Stocking Up

Investing is one way people use their savings to try and earn more money. Many people keep their savings in bank accounts that earn interest. Interest is extra money that the bank adds to the account for letting them use your money for other purposes.

When Bitcoin, a form of virtual money, was first introduced in 2009, stocks sold for $0.09. In 2022, they sold for as high as $18,000.

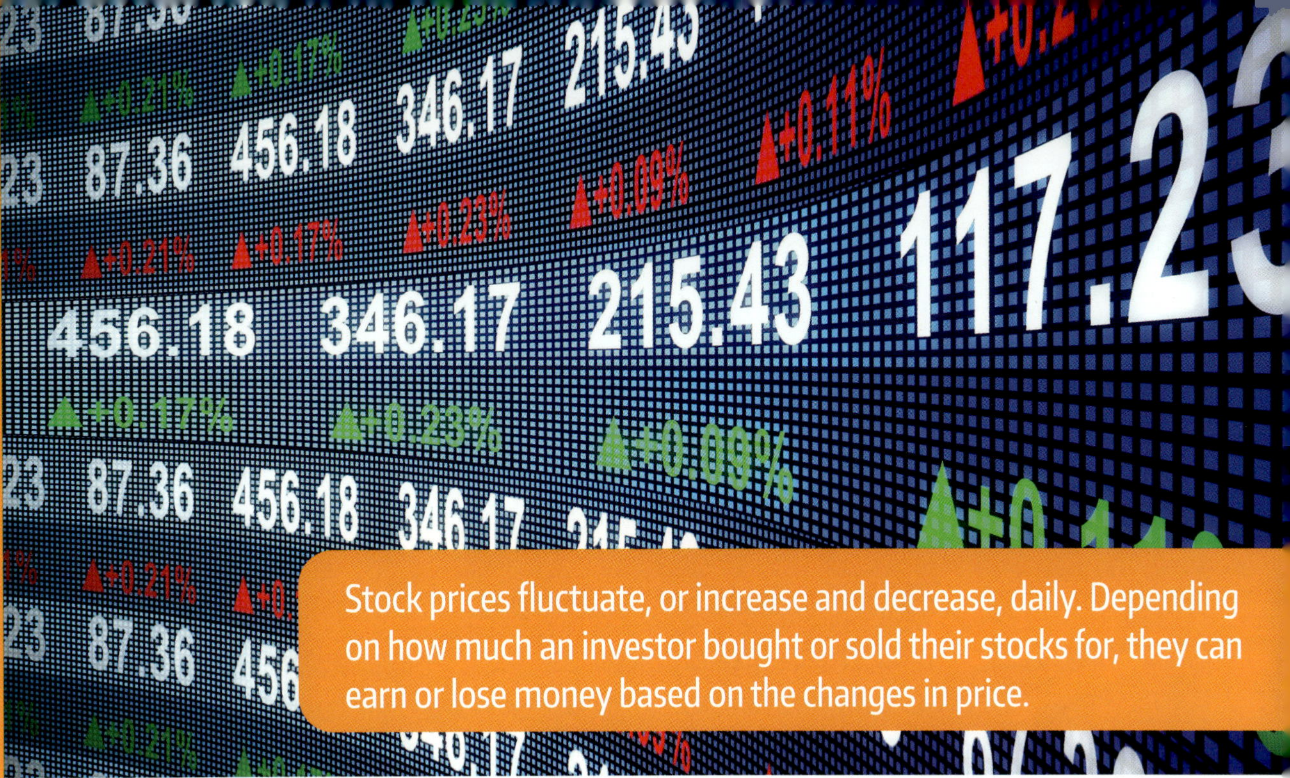

Stock prices fluctuate, or increase and decrease, daily. Depending on how much an investor bought or sold their stocks for, they can earn or lose money based on the changes in price.

Another way to invest is through **stocks**. Investing through stocks comes with risk, or the chance that things will turn out differently than you think. Suppose you invest $100 in the stock of a particular company. If the company's stock price increases and you sell your stock, you receive more than $100. However, if the price decreases and you sell the stock, you receive less than $100.

WORD WISE

A STOCK IS A SHARE IN THE OWNERSHIP OF A COMPANY THAT A PERSON CAN PURCHASE OR SELL. THE STOCK PRICE CAN GO UP OR DOWN DEPENDING ON HOW THE COMPANY IS DOING.

It Makes Cents

It's common for people to save their money for long-term goals, such as college or retirement. For example, some parents put money into special education savings accounts for their children.

College tuition can be very expensive. Having a savings account for college helps people afford to go when they're ready.

Some common retirement savings accounts are 401(k)s, Roth IRAs, and pension funds—to name a few. Each of them has different ways of investing money, such as where they take money from and how much.

People also put their money into retirement funds. Retirement is when you stop working, usually due to old age. You still have expenses, such as food and clothes, but you aren't earning a salary.

Some people place their money into college savings and retirement funds early so they will have money later when they need it.

Consider This

It's common for people to place money from their paychecks into a retirement savings, even if they're not planning on retiring for many years in the future. Why might this be important to do?

Loan on Me

If a person is unable to save their money for expensive things—such as a car or home—they can still get those things by borrowing the money from a bank. This is called taking out a loan.

A loan is very helpful in that you can borrow money to pay for things you want. But paying back the loan when it's time to do so is important.

It's very common for homeowners to borrow money to buy their homes, since homes are so expensive.

People who get loans agree to pay the money back to the bank over time. They also agree to pay a little more than they borrowed. The extra money is called interest. Some loans can be repaid in a short time. Other loans, such as **mortgages**, often take many years to repay. However, the bank may take away the thing a person bought with the loaned money if they fail to repay the loan.

WORD WISE

A MORTGAGE IS A TYPE OF LOAN PEOPLE BORROW TO BUY HOMES. IF THE MORTGAGE ISN'T REPAID, THE LENDER IS ABLE TO TAKE THE PROPERTY FROM THE OWNERS.

Helping Others

There are millions of people around the world who cannot afford food, clothes, housing, and medical care. There are many ways that others can spend some of their own money to help provide these needs.

One way to help is through fundraising, or finding ways to collect money to send to those in need or to buy things they might need. People hold events, such as car washes, bake sales, and raffles, to raise money. A raffle is when people buy tickets for a chance to win prizes.

Fundraising is a great way to earn money for a cause you care about, like new materials for the school's theatre club or a local charity you want to donate to.

A volunteer is someone who willingly offers their time for an activity, such as collecting money to send to victims of natural disasters or serving food at a shelter.

Many people spend money and time helping others. Their actions show kindness, empathy, and compassion. Empathy is a shared understanding of another person's feelings or situation. Compassion is a feeling of concern and care for those who are suffering.

Consider This

Find an organization's website online that helps people in need and find out how you can make a donation. Many organizations have ways to donate directly from their website! Do your research to make sure the organization is real and not an online scam.

Saving the Day

There are many different sources of income: allowances, salaries, gifts, etc. But there are also many expenses, which people pay for with their income. Savings come from income. Savings are set aside for future expenses.

Smart spending includes using coupons and rebates. It's also about comparing prices of goods and services from different sellers and looking for similar items that cost less.

Budgets keep track of your income and expenses. They also show you how to use your savings to afford financial goals. Investing is trying to earn money from your savings.

People make investments for different reasons, like being able to afford long-term financial goals. Saving for college, setting aside money for retirement, and planning to buy a house are long-term goals.

The money you earn pays for goods and services that you need and want. It can also be used to make charitable donations to those in need.

compare and contrast

A habit is something that someone frequently does. How might a teenager's saving and spending habits differ from their parents? How might they be similar?

Setting financial goals can encourage you to save your money and spend less on goods and services you may not really need.

Glossary

advertise Bringing attention to an item or service.
allowance Money given to children at regular times.
bills An amount of money owed for purchasing goods or services.
cashier An employee who handles money and receipts in a store, bank, or other business.
donate To give money or goods as a gift.
exchange To swap one item for another.
goal An object or aim a person plans to buy or achieve over a period of time.
invest Putting money into a savings or bank account with the intention to grow the amount over time.
navigate To figure out.
predict To make a guess about what will happen in the future.
responsible Having a plan and ensuring that you follow it.
scam A false promise or fraud that is harmful to privacy and security.
shipping Having an item sent from a store or warehouse far away to your own home or business, often with additional costs.
spending Using your money to buy goods and services.
variable An amount that can change or vary.

For More Information

Books

Flynn, Sarah Wassner. *Not-So-Common Cents: Super Duper Important Facts About Money You Can't Afford to Miss.* Washington, D.C.: National Geographic Kids, 2023.

Jackson, Ty Allan, and Nicole Miles. *Make Your Own Money: How Kids Can Earn It, Save It, Spend It, and Dream Big, with Danny Dollar, the King of Cha-Ching*. North Adams, MA: Storey Publishing LLC, 2021.

Nhin, Mary. *Money Ninja: A Children's Book About Saving, Investing, and Donating*. Edmond, OK: Grow Grit Press LLC, 2020.

Websites

Economics

jr.brainpop.com/socialstudies/economics/

Learn more about goods and services and needs and wants through informative videos and fun games.

Saving and Spending

jr.brainpop.com/socialstudies/economics/savingandspending/

Games and activities about saving and spending can be found here.

Publisher's note to educators and parents: Our editors have carefully reviewed these websites to ensure that they are suitable for students. Many websites change frequently, however, and we cannot guarantee that a site's future contents will continue to meet our high standards of quality and educational value. Be advised that students should be closely supervised whenever they access the internet.

Index